The Skateboarder's Guide to
Skate Parks, Half-Pipes, Bowls, and Obstacles™

AWESOME OBSTACLES

How to Build Your Own Skateboard Ramps and Ledges

Justin Hocking

The Rosen Publishing Group, Inc., New York

For Matt and Sean

Published in 2005 by The Rosen Publishing Group, Inc.
29 East 21st Street, New York, NY 10010

Copyright © 2005 by The Rosen Publishing Group, Inc.

First Edition

Library of Congress Cataloging-in-Publication Data

Hocking, Justin.
Awesome obstacles: how to build your own skateboard ramps and ledges/Justin Hocking.—1st ed.
    p. cm.—(The skateboarder's guide to skate parks, half-pipes, bowls, and obstacles)
Includes bibliographical references and index.
ISBN 1-4042-0337-0 (library binding)
1. Skateboarding—Juvenile literature.
I. Title. II. Series.
GV859.8.H6 2005
796.22—dc22

                                                                    2004012881

Manufactured in the United States of America

On the cover: Skaters sitting on a completed jump ramp

CONTENTS

INTRODUCTION

Skateboarding is a creative sport. When you skate, there aren't any coaches telling you how to train or which tricks to do. Because there are no fixed routines, you get to choose how and where you ride. Skaters aren't confined to courts or playing fields, so they search for skate spots in unlikely places like parking lots, sidewalks, and urban office plazas. Unfortunately, business owners and city officials will do just about anything to keep you from skateboarding on their property or in public areas.

Bank ramps, like the one shown here, are relatively easy obstacles to build. They are also perfect for doing all types of tricks, from the most basic to the more advanced.

They put up "no skateboarding" signs. They install skatestoppers— those annoying little metal brackets and knobs designed to prevent skating on ledges and rails. They even hire private security guards to chase skaters away.

It can be tough to find decent places to skate, but with a little hard work, you can actually create your own skate spots. That's right. If you have access to a few tools and the right materials, you can actually build your own obstacles. That way, you don't have to spend so much time searching for skate spots, and you don't have to worry about trespassing on anyone's private property. You just walk out the front door and you're ready to roll. If you make several obstacles, you can even set up your own private skate park. And during the process, you're guaranteed to learn a lot about carpentry, math, problem solving, and, of course, skateboarding itself.

This book will help you build a few different types of skating obstacles, including manual pads, slider bars, bank ramps, fun boxes, and jump ramps. We'll talk about everything you need to know to build your own skate creations, including tips on safety, materials, tools, and maintaining your obstacles.

CHAPTER 1

Safety and Adult Supervision

This book is designed to help you build your own obstacles, but that doesn't mean you should try to do everything on your own. The truth is that working with wood and certain tools can be dangerous. And you always need to work under the close supervision of an adult with carpentry experience. If you do decide to build one of the obstacles described in this book, ask a parent, relative, woodshop teacher, or local carpenter for help.

Most of the obstacles in this book can be built using nonelectrical tools, such as handheld saws and ordinary hammers. On the other hand, you can build things in half the time and with more precision if you use electrical power tools, like a circular saw, which we'll discuss later in this chapter. If you do decide to use power tools, they should be handled only by an experienced adult. Below are some other important safety tips.

1. Always use eye protection, like sunglasses or goggles, when using any tool.
2. Keep your work site clean. Don't leave scrap lumber lying around because you could trip on it.
3. Never leave a piece of wood lying around that has a nail sticking out of it. Someone might step on it.
4. When lifting heavy objects, bend your knees and use your legs, instead of your back, to lift.
5. When setting down heavy objects, watch out for your fingers and toes.
6. If you start to feel tired, stop and take a rest.
7. Make sure to keep power tools and electrical cords away from water and out of the rain.
8. Once you finish your obstacle and actually start skating on it, make sure to wear all the proper safety equipment, like a helmet, elbow pads, and knee pads.

Tools

Since the structures explained in this book are all fairly simple to create, chances are good your parents might already own some or all the tools you'll need. If you don't own some of these tools, you can try borrowing them from friends or relatives.

Tools are expensive, so it's important to take good care of them. Never leave any tool lying on the ground. Store them in the proper place, such as a shed or garage. On the next page is a list of some tools you may need.

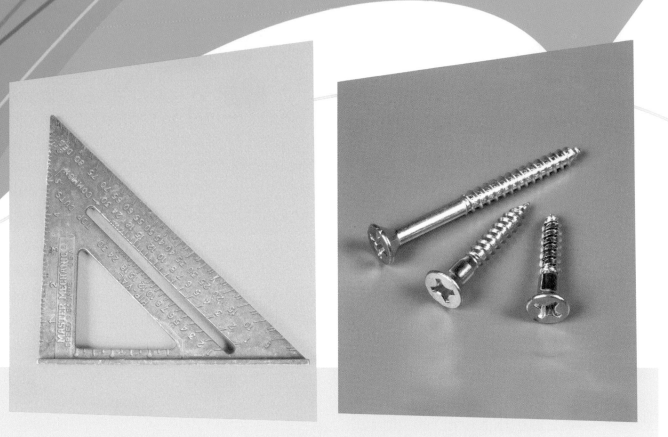

The speed square *(left)* and screws of various sizes *(right)* are some of the tools and materials you'll be using for your project.

1. **Tape measure:** Since a tape measure can be wound up into a compact unit, it's more convenient than a regular wooden or metal ruler.
2. **Speed square:** This triangular metal tool can be used to measure right angles on your lumber before you cut it.
3. **Hammer:** A hammer is essential because nails are used to hold each of the obstacles together.
4. **Drill:** A drill is also essential because screws are used throughout the building process. The different attachments you put on a drill are called bits.

5. **Phillips-head bit:** This bit for the drill is used for driving screws with a Phillips head (a Phillips head looks like a small plus sign).
6. **Countersink bit:** This large drill bit is used for making countersinking holes (we'll talk about countersinking later on).
7. **Extension bit:** This very long drill bit is used for drilling in hard-to-reach places, like the inside of a round pipe.
8. **Pry bar:** This long, thin tool with a forked end is used for prying nails from wood. It's also known as a crowbar.
9. **Handsaw:** A handsaw is important because you'll need to cut a lot of lumber.
10. **Carpentry pencil:** This thick pencil is used specially for marking on lumber.
11. **Circular saw:** Also called a skill saw, a circular saw is an electric power tool with a circular blade, used for cutting lumber quickly and precisely.
12. **Jigsaw:** This is another type of electrical power saw with a short, straight blade. It is slower than a circular saw but sometimes more precise and better for cutting irregular shapes like curves and circles.
13. **Caulk:** Caulk is another word for a heavy-duty carpenter's glue. Caulk comes in long tubes, and you have to use a caulk gun to squeeze it out.

Materials

Here are some of the materials you might need.

1. **Two-by-four:** A two-by-four is a thin wooden board that's commonly used in carpentry. Even though it's called a two-by-four, it's actually approximately 1½ inches (38 mm) tall and 3½ inches (89 mm) wide, but it's easier to just call it a two-by-four.

Lumberyards sell two-by-fours in all different lengths, but the most common is an 8-foot (2.4 m) length, also called a stud.

2. **Two-by-six:** This is another type of wooden board that's about 2 inches (51 mm) tall and 6 inches (0.15 m) wide.

3. **Four-by-four:** Much thicker than two-by-fours or two-by-sixes, four-by-fours, which are 4 inches (0.1 m) tall and 4 inches (0.1 m) wide, are often used as posts to hold up heavy structures.

4. **Plywood:** Plywood is a building material made of long, thin layers of wood glued tightly together. Plywood is typically sold in sheets that are 4 feet (1.2 m) wide and 8 feet (2.4 m) long, and that have a variety of different thicknesses. This is where knowing your fractions comes in handy: ¾-inch-thick (19 mm) plywood is the thickest that these projects require, while ⅜-inch-thick (9.5 mm) plywood is much thinner.

5. **Masonite:** Since plywood tends to wear out and splinter quickly, many people place a type of smooth surfacing called Masonite as the top layer of their ramps and obstacles. Masonite is relatively cheap—usually under $20 per sheet. Like plywood, Masonite comes in several different thicknesses. For some of the obstacles in this book, use thick Masonite.

6. **Skatelite:** Skatelite is a new, highly durable type of Masonite, which is made from a mixture of wood and plastic. Though it's the best surface you can buy, at upward of $100 per sheet it's expensive. It might be worth the investment, though. It will last for years and years.

7. **Coping:** Coping is the round metal pipe placed on top of ramps, which is used for grinds and slides.

When choosing building materials, the two main factors to consider are cost and quality. Lumber can be expensive. Prices vary, depending

For your safety, get some thick work gloves *(left)* that fit your hands snugly to prevent cuts and splinters from jagged edges. You will also need some dust masks *(center)* so that you don't breathe in toxic dust and goggles *(right)* to protect your eyes from flying bits of construction material.

on the season and demand. Look in the classifieds for people selling scrap lumber, or search the Internet or yellow pages for lumberyards that sell used wood. Stop by construction sites and ask workers if they have any scrap lumber. Keep your eyes out for sales at the local lumber shop or discount stores like Home Depot.

When you purchase lumber, you need to check out the quality first, the same way you check out a new skateboard deck before you buy it. When buying two-by-fours, like buying skateboard decks, the most important thing to look for is warpage. Most boards have a slight curve. That's fine, but avoid severely warped boards. If it's in the shape of a rainbow, put it back in the pile. You have to make sure you get quality wood because once you use it, you can't take it back. Also, for skateboard obstacles, always buy exterior grade lumber, which is much cheaper than interior grade (it's called interior grade because it's used inside houses).

Getting Started

Don't just jump into a building project without doing some serious planning first. There's nothing worse than starting a project you can't finish. We suggest you read this whole book first and then decide which obstacle might be best for your situation. Here are some important things to consider before you begin.

1. **Space:** How much room do you have? Will you be skating in the street or in the driveway? If you live in the middle of a big city, building a large bank ramp or fun box might end up being more trouble than it's worth.
2. **Parents:** Without your parents' approval, it's no go.
3. **Cost:** How much money can you spend? If you buy all new lumber, even a small manual pad can cost around $40 to build. A fun box, depending on the size, can cost more than $100 to build. These are just estimates, though. We've included material lists for each obstacle, so it's up to you to call around and see what the going rate is for all the materials you need. It's important to do this kind of pricing before you get started. If you build something you can't afford to complete, you'll end up with nothing but an unusable pile of junk and a big hole in your pocket.
4. **Portability:** Do you want something you can move around easily? If so, you might consider a smaller obstacle like a slider bar or a manual pad.

WHAT'S COUNTERSINKING?

Countersinking sounds like something you'd do in the kitchen, right? Actually, countersinking means using a drill to enlarge the top part of a hole so that the screw head will lie just below the surface.

Whenever you use Masonite or Skatelite, you should always use your large countersink bit to make some shallow holes before you actually screw the sheet to the frame of your obstacle. It sounds like a lot of extra work, but there's a very good reason for countersinking. If your screw heads stick up even slightly above the surface, your clothing or skin can get caught on them when you fall, which can lead to serious injuries.

Once you actually start building an obstacle, you'll discover that building things requires a lot of problem-solving skills. It can be frustrating, but it's also a great learning experience. You may run into problems that aren't addressed in this book. Use your common sense and come up with creative solutions. If that doesn't work, ask an expert.

CHAPTER 2

How to Build a Manual Pad

A manual pad is a low, flat platform that's used for manual tricks. (A manual is a trick in which you lift your front trucks up and balance on your back wheels only. Nose manuals are another variation where you balance on your front wheels only.)

Manual pads are relatively lightweight and fairly portable. And they're pretty easy to build, too. All you really have to do is construct a large rectangular box. The top of the box acts as a low platform on which you can do a number of manual tricks.

Dimensions

4 inches (0.1 m) tall, 4 feet (1.2 m) wide, 8 feet (2.4 m) long

Materials

- 1 pound (0.45 kg) of 2½-inch (64 mm) wood screws
- 1 pound (0.45 kg) of nails
- (1) 4 foot x 8 foot (1.2 m x 2.4 m) sheet of ¼-inch-thick (6 mm) Masonite or Skatelite (optional)
- (1) 8 foot (2.5 m) length of 2 inch x 2 inch (51 mm x 51 mm) angle iron (optional)
- (1) 4 foot x 8 foot (1.2 m x 2.4 m) sheet of ¾-inch-thick (19 mm) plywood
- (3) 8-foot-long (2.4 m) two-by-fours

How It's Done

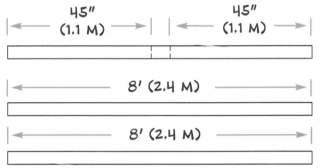

MANUAL PAD

1

The first thing you need to do is cut one of your two-by-fours into two 45-inch (1.1 m) pieces. Lay out one of your two-by-fours and measure out 45 inches (1.1 m) with your tape measure. Mark the 45-inch (1.1 m) spot with your pencil. Then turn the two-by-four around and measure 45 inches (1.1 m) from the other end and make another mark. Use your speed square to pencil in straight lines across the two-by-four at each 45-inch (1.1 m) mark. This straight line will act as a guide to help you make straight cuts with your saw.

After cutting the two 45-inch (1.1 m) pieces, check to make sure the two other two-by-fours are exactly 8 feet (2.4 m) long. Some lumberyards cut their 8-foot (2.4 m) two-by-fours at slightly irregular lengths. If so, cut the end off to make them both exactly 8 feet (2.4 m) long.

(continued on page 16)

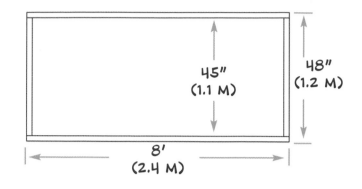

2 Now lay out all four of your two-by-fours in the shape of your box. The two 45-inch (1.1 m) pieces should go on the inside of the longer pieces, so that your box is exactly 48 inches (1.2 m) wide. As we mentioned earlier, a two-by-four is actually about 1½ inches (38 mm) tall. So the width of two two-by-fours is 3 inches (76 mm), which, when added to your 45-inch (1.1 m) pieces, is exactly 48 inches (1.2 m). Now use nails or screws to fasten all the pieces of your box together.

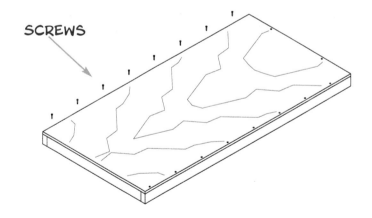

SCREWS

3 Once the frame of your box is done, it's time to add the plywood. Your 4-foot-by-8-foot (1.2 m by 2.4 m) sheet should fit perfectly on top. Lay it down flat on the box frame. Then attach it to the framework with wood screws. If you decide to add a layer of Masonite on top, countersink some holes before you attach it to the layer of plywood. Then attach the Masonite using 1¼-inch (31.8 mm) screws. Congratulations! Your manual pad is now ready to skate.

MANUAL PAD

OVERALL DIMENSIONS
4 inches (0.1 m) tall
4 feet (1.2 m) wide
8 feet (2.4 m) long

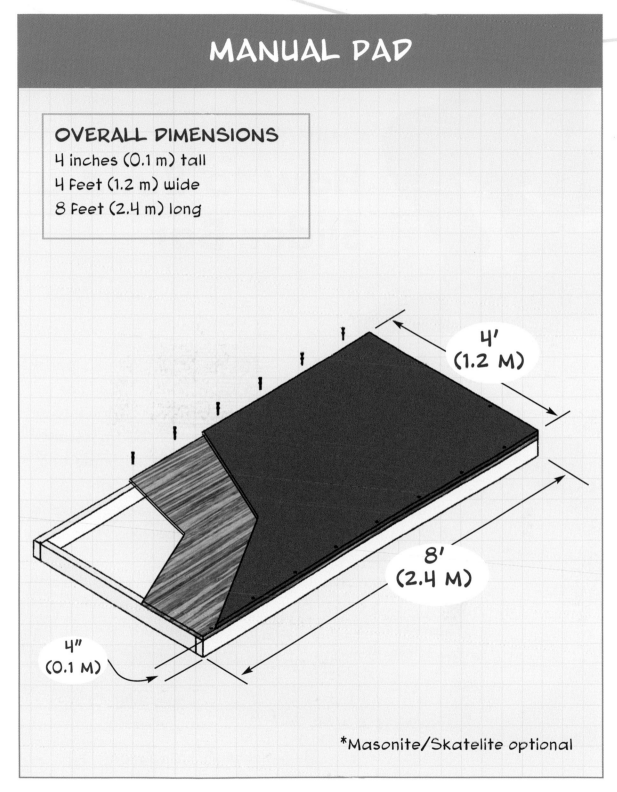

4'
(1.2 M)

8'
(2.4 M)

4"
(0.1 M)

*Masonite/Skatelite optional

CHAPTER 3

How to Build a Slider Bar

A slider bar is a long, thin obstacle that's perfect for boardslides and grinds. The slider bar is the easiest and least expensive obstacle to build of the obstacles discussed in this book. It's also the most portable—dragging it around is simple and it fits in most cars. Since the slider bar is so light and portable, you can bring it almost anywhere. It's perfect to bring to an empty parking lot, where you can have a skate session with your friends.

Another advantage of the slider bar is that the coping allows you to do grinds and slides easily. It's much harder to do these tricks on a rough curb. And you won't be damaging public property either.

Dimensions

8 feet (2.4 m) long, 6 inches (0.15 m) high

Materials

- ½ pound (0.2 kg) of 1½-inch-long (38 mm) wood screws
- ½ pound (0.2 kg) of nails
- (2) 8-foot-long (2.4 m) two-by-fours
- (1) 8-foot-long (2.4 m) two-by-six
- (2) 8-foot (2.4 m) lengths of 2¾-inch-thick (69.9 mm) steel coping

How It's Done

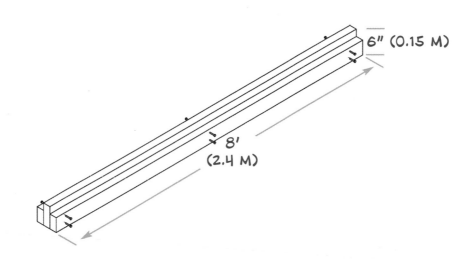

6" (0.15 M)

8'
(2.4 M)

SLIDER BAR

1

Find a very flat surface, like a garage floor, to lay out your lumber. Place all three pieces of wood on their skinny edge, with the two-by-six placed in between the two two-by-fours. Push all the lumber tightly together, like making a really long submarine sandwich (the two-by-fours are like the bread, and the two-by-six is like the meat).

Now nail the two-by-fours to both sides of the two-by-six. Make sure the bottom edges of all the boards are perfectly aligned when you nail them together, so that the finished product will sit flat on the ground.

(continued on page 20)

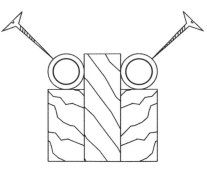

2

Now you need to attach both pieces of coping on each side of the two-by-six and on top of the two-by-fours. This is where you need a power drill with a countersink bit and a 3-inch-long (76.2 mm) extension bit. Using your countersink bit, drill a large hole all the way through the coping. Then, just behind this large hole on the inside of the coping, drill a smaller hole one that's just big enough for the sharp part of the screw to fit.

Now use your extension bit to pass a screw all the way through the large hole, and then to screw the coping to the two-by-six through the smaller hole. Once your coping is firmly attached, your bar is ready for some serious slides and grinds.

SLIDER BAR

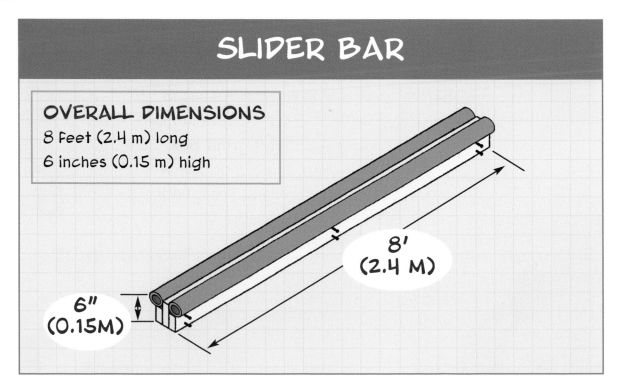

OVERALL DIMENSIONS
8 feet (2.4 m) long
6 inches (0.15 m) high

8'
(2.4 M)

6"
(0.15M)

CHAPTER 4

How to Build a Grind Box

A grind box is very similar to a manual pad, but it's usually taller and thinner than a standard manual pad. To build a grind box, you basically build the frames for two small manual pads and then attach them with short two-by-fours.

It's a good idea to build a regular manual pad before you build a grind box, just to get the hang of carpentry. In fact, an already-built manual pad can even be converted into a grind box. So if you've already built your manual pad but would rather have a grind box, you've already begun the process.

Dimensions

1 foot 3 inches (0.38 m) tall, 1 foot 4 inches (0.4 m) wide, 6 feet (1.8 m) long

Materials

- 1 pound (0.45 kg) of 2½-inch-long (64 mm) wood screws
- 1 pound (0.45 kg) of nails
- 1 tube of construction grade caulk/adhesive
- 1 caulk gun
- (6) 8-foot-long (2.4 m) two-by-fours
- (1) 4-foot-by-8-foot (1.2 m by 2.4 m) sheet of ¾-inch-thick (19 mm) plywood
- (2) 8-foot-long (2.4 m) 2 inch x 2 inch (51 mm x 51 mm) angle irons/coping edge

How It's Done

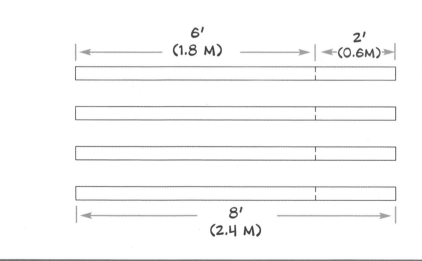

First, lay all your lumber out so you can measure everything. Measure and cut four of the two-by-fours down from 8 feet (2.4 m) to 6 feet (1.8 m) (the length of your grind box). Check out the first step in chapter 2 for instructions on measuring and cutting your two-by-fours.

GRIND BOX

1

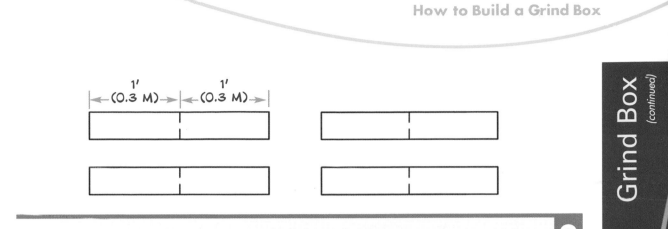

2

Now take the four short pieces of leftover wood from your first cut and measure and cut each into two 1-foot (0.3 m) sections.

Next, measure and cut one of the 8-foot (2.4 m) two-by-fours into six sections that are each 1 foot 4 inches (0.4 m) long. You'll get all six pieces from one two-by-four.

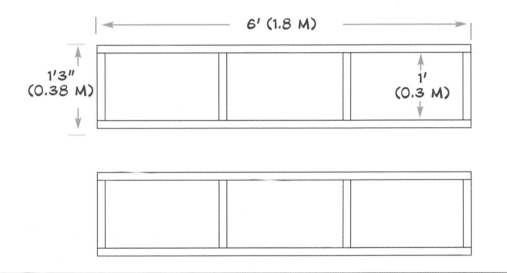

3

As we mentioned before, you're basically building two manual pads and connecting them with two-by-fours. So take two of your 1-foot (0.3 m) two-by-four sections and nail them to two of your 6-foot (1.8 m) two-by-four sections, forming a large rectangle (just like the manual pad in chapter 2, but not as wide). Use your tape measure and make a mark on each side of the box at 2 feet (0.6 m) and 4 feet (1.2 m). Add another 1-foot (0.3 m) section of two-by-four at each set of marks. Adding these extra supports will make your grind box more sturdy. Repeat these last two steps so that you have two separate frames.

(continued on page 24)

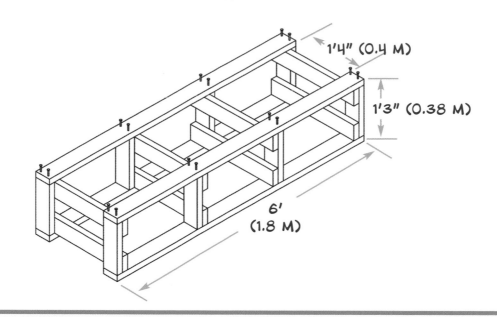

1'4" (0.4 M)

1'3" (0.38 M)

6'
(1.8 M)

4

Set the frames on their sides, about 1 foot 4 inches (0.4 m) apart. Use the 1-foot-4-inch (0.4 m) sections of two-by-four to attach the two frames. Four of the 16-inch (0.4 m) sections will attach the boxes at the corners. Place one of these vertical supports at the 2-foot (0.6 m) mark, and then the other at the 4-foot (1.2 m) mark. Make sure your vertical supports are flush (which is another word for "even") with the top and bottom frames.

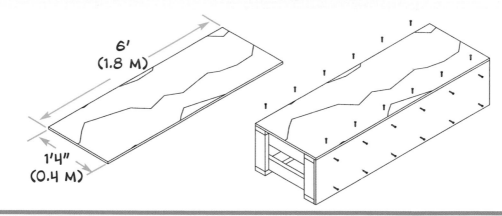

6'
(1.8 M)

1'4"
(0.4 M)

5

Now you need to measure out and cut one piece of plywood that is 1 foot 4 inches (0.4 m) wide and 6 feet (1.8 m) long (and two that are each 1 foot 3 inches (0.38 m) wide and 6 feet (1.8 m). Cutting plywood with a handsaw can be difficult and time consuming, so if possible have an adult make these cuts with a circular saw. Now screw the plywood down on the side and top of the box, just like wrapping a present.

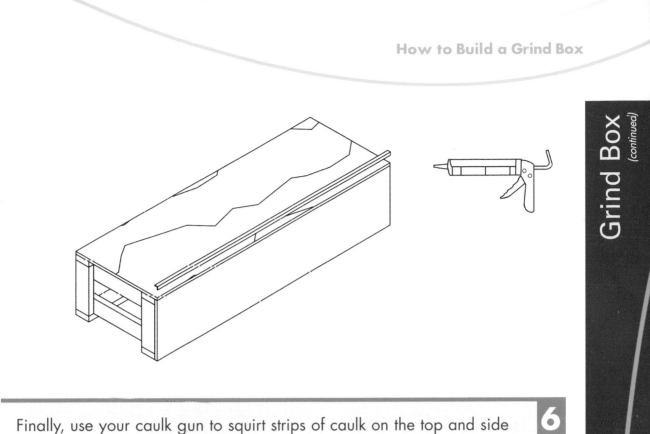

6 Finally, use your caulk gun to squirt strips of caulk on the top and side edges of the box. Slap the angle iron pieces in place, wait for the caulk to dry, and you're ready to grind!

Congratulations! Your grind box is complete—see page 26 for the finished drawing. Like the slider bar, the grind box is relatively portable. So bring it to a local parking lot (empty, of course) and test it out.

GRIND BOX

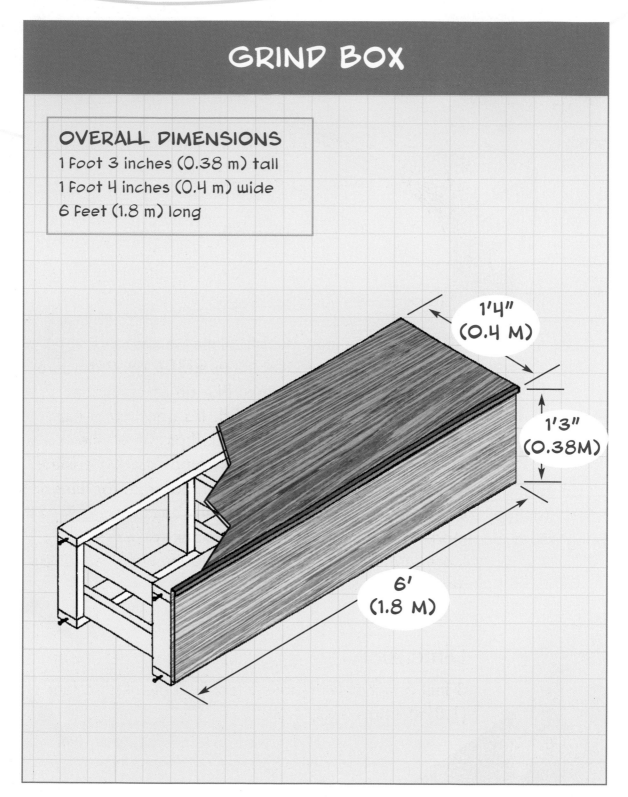

OVERALL DIMENSIONS
1 Foot 3 inches (0.38 m) tall
1 Foot 4 inches (0.4 m) wide
6 Feet (1.8 m) long

1'4"
(0.4 M)

1'3"
(0.38M)

6'
(1.8 M)

CHAPTER 5

How to Build a Bank Ramp

A bank ramp is a small, wedge-shaped structure with a slanted face, like an embankment, after which it's named. It's good for a variety of tricks, like ollies and kick flips. Of all the different types of ramps, bank ramps are the easiest to build and are also one of the most fun. Building a bank ramp is a good step toward building other, more difficult ramps. From the bank ramp, you'll learn the steps necessary to build even bigger ramps like half-pipes.

Dimensions

3 feet 6 inches (1 m) tall, 6 feet (1.8 m) wide, 6 feet (1.8 m) long

Materials

- 2 pounds (0.9 kg) of 2½-inch-long (64 mm) wood screws
- 1 pound (0.45 kg) of 1¼-inch-long (32 mm) wood screws
- (11) 8-foot-long (2.4 m) two-by-fours
- (2) 4 foot x 8 foot (1.2 m x 2.4 m) sheets of ¼-inch-thick (6 mm) Masonite or Skatelite
- (3) 4 foot x 8 foot (1.2 m x 2.4 m) sheets of ¾-inch-thick (19 mm) plywood

How It's Done

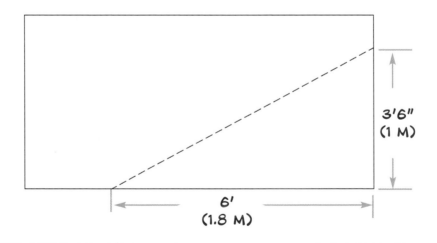

**3'6"
(1 M)**

**6'
(1.8 M)**

BANK RAMP

1

The first task is to measure and cut the triangular sidewalls (also known as templates) of your bank ramp. Find a flat surface and lay one piece of your ¾-inch-thick (19 mm) plywood down on the ground. Use your tape measure and pencil to make a mark on the short edge of the plywood a 3 feet 6 inches (1 m), and another on the long edge at 6 feet (1.8 m).

Now lay one of your two-by-fours between the two marks, and use it as a straight edge to draw a line with your pencil, connecting the marks. Now you have the outline of your triangle.

Next, cut along the line you've just drawn. For the best results, have an adult make the cut with an electrical circular saw.

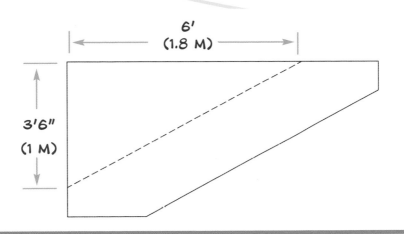

6'
(1.8 M)

3'6"
(1 M)

2

Since your bank ramp will have two sidewalls, take your first triangle, flip it over, and retrace it on the leftover part of the same piece of plywood. That way, you'll save lumber and your sidewalls will be exactly the same size and shape.

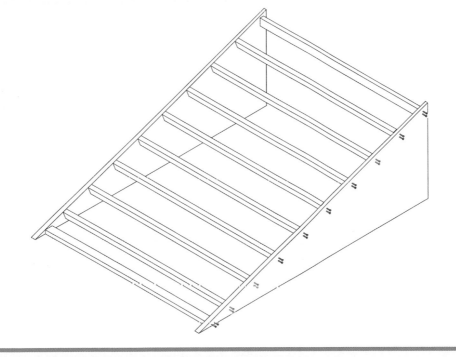

3

Make marks on all your two-by-fours at 5 feet 10½ inches (1.79 m). Once you're finished, go ahead and make all ten cuts. There will be one cross support about every 10¼ inches (0.26 m), so "sandwich" your two sidewalls together, and use your tape measure and pencil to make marks every 10¼ inches (0.26 m) on the slanted edges.

(continued on page 30)

Now separate your sidewalls and stand them on edge (this will be much easier if you have a couple of friends to help). Begin screwing eight of the two-by-fours in at each 10¼-inch (0.26 m) mark, with the skinny side of the two-by-four facing upward and perfectly even (or flush) with the face edge of the plywood. Use the longer, 2½-inch (64 mm) screws to attach the cross supports. Drive the screws in from the outside face of the template, putting in two screws on each end (a total of four screws for each two-by-four). The other two joists, or cross supports, should be screwed in at the bottom of the ramp, flush with the ground. One goes at the tip of the bank, while the other one goes in the very back.

4

Now measure out your plywood. On the first piece, you simply need to measure 6 feet 10 inches (2 m) up, and trim off the top. The next piece will also be 6 feet 10 inches (2 m) long, but you need to cut it in half, so it will cover the remaining 2 feet (0.6 m) of the 6-foot-wide (1.8 m) ramp.

Once you've cut your plywood, lay it lengthwise on the bank ramp and begin attaching it with your drill and the 2½-inch (64 mm) wood screws. Using the screw heads in the sidewalls as a guide, draw straight lines across the top of the plywood, exactly above several of the cross supports. Use this line as a guide for drilling in the screws, so that each screw will actually catch on the two-by-four cross supports below.

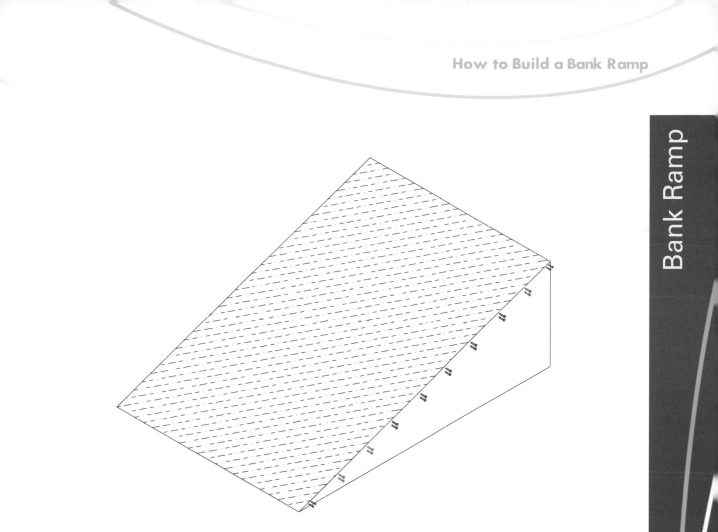

5

Now measure and cut 2 feet (0.6 m) off the length of both your pieces of Masonite. Then cut 14 inches (0.36 m) off the side of one of the pieces so it's exactly 34 inches (0.86 m) wide.

Using just a couple of screws, attach your Masonite to the ramp. Before you screw in the rest of the sheet, you need to make countersink holes so that the screw heads won't stick out above the Masonite. Just like when attaching the plywood, use the screw heads in the sidewalls as a guide and draw a straight line across the top of the Masonite, exactly above several of the cross supports. This line is a guide that shows you exactly where to make countersink holes.

Now attach the Masonite using 1¼-inch (31.8 mm) screws and then you're good to go. See page 32 for the finished drawing.

BANK RAMP

OVERALL DIMENSIONS

3 Feet 6 inches (1 m) tall
6 Feet (1.8 m) wide
6 Feet (1.8 m) long

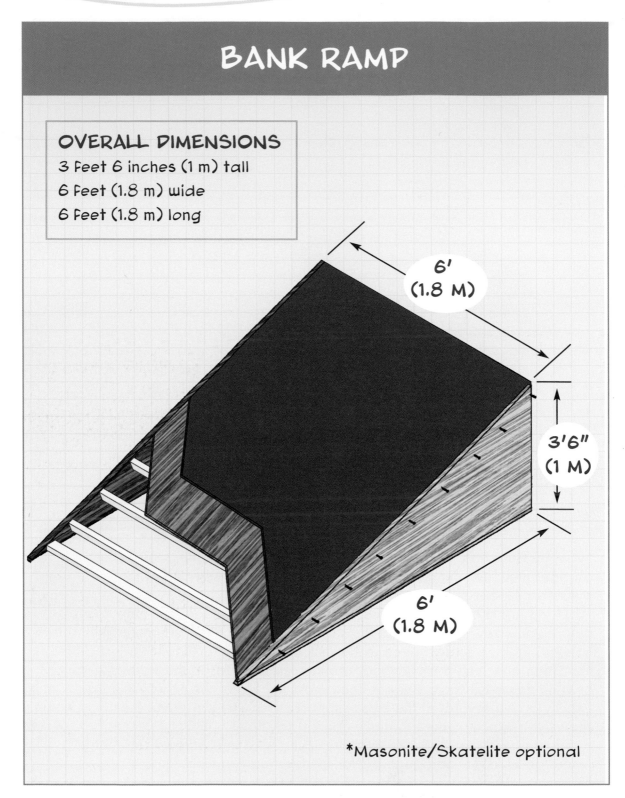

6'
(1.8 M)

3'6"
(1 M)

6'
(1.8 M)

*Masonite/Skatelite optional

CHAPTER 6

How to Build a Fun Box

A fun box is basically just two bank ramps with a tall manual pad in the middle. They're good for ollies and manuals, or you can even place a slider bar on top. If you already have a manual pad, you can elevate it and place it between two bank ramps. If not, just build one from scratch.

Dimensions

Each bank is 4 feet (1.2 m) wide, 2 feet 9½ inches (0.85 m) high, and 7 feet 6 inches (2.29 m) long. The box is 4 feet (1.2 m) wide, 2 feet 9½ inches (0.85 m) high, and 8 feet (2.4 m) long.

Materials

- 2½ pounds (1.13 kg) of 2½-inch-long (64 mm) wood screws

- 2 pounds (0.9 kg) of 1¼-inch-long (32 mm) wood screws
- 1 pound (0.45 kg) of nails
- (14) 8-foot-long (2.4 m) two-by-fours
- (3) 4 foot x 8 foot (1.2 m x 2.4 m) sheets of ¼-inch-thick (6 mm) Masonite or Skatelite (optional)
- (4) 4 foot x 8 foot (1.2 m x 2.4 m) sheets of ¾-inch-thick (19 mm) plywood
- (2) 8-foot-long (2.4 m) four-by-fours

How It's Done

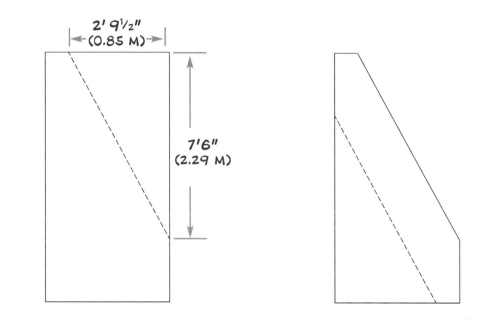

1

Just like when building the larger bank ramp in the last section, the first task is to measure and cut the triangular sidewalls, or templates, of your bank ramp. Find a flat surface and lay one piece of your ¾-inch-thick (19 mm) plywood down on the ground. Use your tape measure and pencil to make a mark on the short edge of the plywood at 2 feet 9½ inches (0.85 m), and another on the long edge at 7 feet 6 inches (2.29 m). Use one of your two-by-fours as a straight edge to connect the two marks with a thick pencil mark.

Now you have the outline of your triangle. The next step is to cut along the line you've just drawn. Since your bank ramp will have two sidewalls, take your first triangle, flip it over, and retrace it on the leftover part of the same piece of plywood.

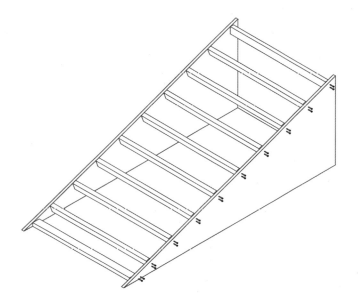

2

Now you need to make 11 two-by-four joists to connect your templates. Each cross support will be 3 feet 10½ inches (1.18 m), so if you measure and mark 3 feet 10½ inches (1.18 m) from each end of an 8-foot (2.4 m) two-by-four, you'll get two cross supports from each board. There will be one cross support about every 10 inches (0.25 m), so sandwich your two sidewalls together and use your tape measure and pencil to make marks every 10 inches (0.25 m) on the slanted edge.

Now separate your sidewalls and stand them on edge. Begin screwing the two-by-fours in at each 10-inch (0.25 m) mark, with the skinny side of the two-by-four facing upward and perfectly flush with the face edge of the plywood.

Use the longer 2½-inch (64 mm) screws to attach the cross supports. You should screw from the outside face of the template, putting in two screws on each end (a total of 4 screws for each two-by-four). The other two joists should be screwed in at the bottom of the ramp, flush with the ground. One goes at the tip of the bank, while the other one goes in the very back.

(continued on page 36)

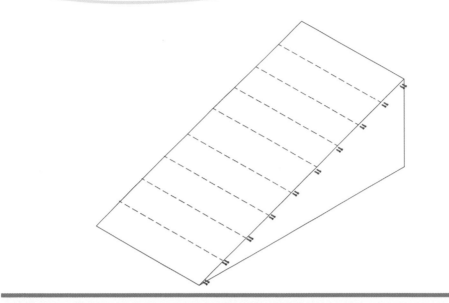

3

Once your bank ramp frame is done, it's time to add the plywood. If you've done everything correctly up to this point, your 8-foot piece of ¾-inch (19 mm) plywood will fit perfectly on the ramp. Lay it lengthwise up the frame.

Then, using the screw heads in the sidewalls as a guide, draw a straight lines across the top of the plywood, exactly above several of the cross supports. Use this line as a guide for drilling in the 2½-inch-long (64 mm) screws, so that each screw will actually catch on the two-by-four cross supports below. Since you need two bank ramps of exactly the same size, simply repeat the past three steps.

NOTE;
MANUAL PAD SHOWN HERE UPSIDE DOWN

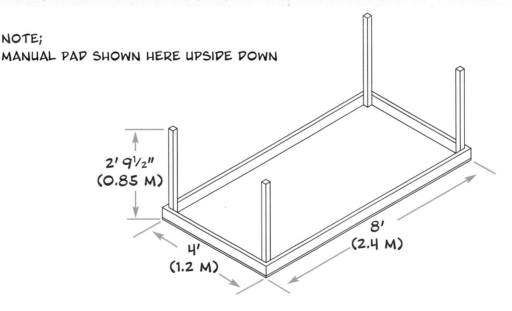

2' 9½"
(0.85 M)

4'
(1.2 M)

8'
(2.4 M)

4

Follow the directions in the manual pad section to build an 8-foot (2.4 m) manual pad. Or, if you choose, you can make the box 6 feet (1.82 m) long, which will make it easier to jump over the whole fun box, from ramp to ramp.

The next step is to elevate your manual pad to the exact same size of the top of your bank ramps, which are 2 feet 9½ inches (0.85 m) high. So you need to cut your four-by-fours down into 4 pieces, each 2 feet 9½ inches (0.85 m) high. Since four-by-fours are much thicker, they're more difficult to cut. The best method for cutting four-by-fours is with a circular saw, so ask for help from a parent or other adult.

Now place one 2-foot-9½-inch (0.85 m) four-by-four in the inside corner of your manual pad frame. Use a drill and some 2½-inch (64 mm) wood screws to attach each four-by-four to the outer frame of the box.

5

Now simply slide the three pieces together, with one bank ramp on either end of your elevated manual pad. If you want, you can use screws to fasten the three sections. Or, you can leave them unattached, which allows you to move the pieces around in different configurations. For instance, you can push the bank ramps together, back to back, to form an angled jump. See page 38 for the finished drawing.

FUN BOX

OVERALL DIMENSIONS

BANK RAMPS

2 feet 9½ inches (0.85 m) tall

4 feet (1.2 m) wide

7 feet 6 inches (2.29 m) long

ELEVATED MANUAL PAD

2 feet 9½ inches (0.85 m) tall

4 feet (1.2 m) wide

8 feet (2.4 m) long

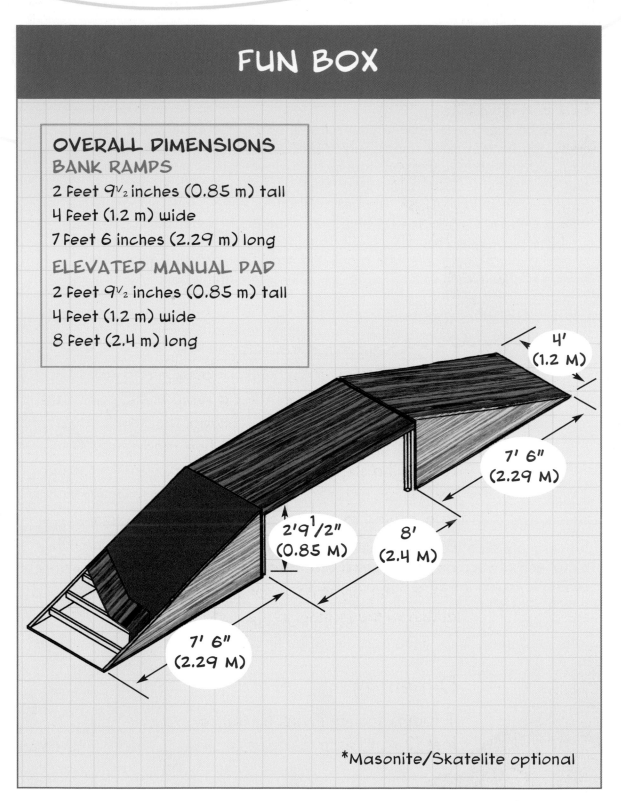

4'
(1.2 M)

7' 6"
(2.29 M)

2'9¹/2"
(0.85 M)

8'
(2.4 M)

7' 6"
(2.29 M)

*Masonite/Skatelite optional

CHAPTER 7

How to Build a Jump Ramp

Jump ramps are small, portable ramps used for launching airs. Building a jump ramp is similar to building a bank ramp, except the face of the ramp is curved instead of flat (we recommend you review the steps for building a bank ramp before you try a jump ramp). Since you have to attach plywood to a curved face, you should use two sheets of thinner, ⅜-inch-thick (9.5 mm) plywood, which is much easier to bend than thicker ¾-inch (19 mm) plywood. The thinner plywood is, of course, easier to bend and attach to the contour of the face of the ramp.

Dimensions

1 foot 6 inches (0.46 m) tall, 4 feet (1.2 m) wide, 8 feet (2.4 m) long

Materials

- 3½ pounds (1.59 kg) of 2½-inch-long (64 mm) wood screws
- 1 pound (0.45 kg) of 1¼-inch-long (32 mm) wood screws
- (6) 8-foot-long (2.4 m) two-by-fours
- (2) 4 foot x 8 foot (1.2 m x 2.4 m) sheets of ⅜-inch-thick (9.5 mm) plywood
- (1) 4 x 8 (1.2 m x 2.4 m) sheet of ¾-inch-thick (19 mm) plywood
- (1) 4 x 8 (1.2 m x 2.4 m) sheet of ¼-inch-thick (.6 mm) Masonite or Skatelite

How It's Done

Building a jump ramp can be broken down into three separate steps: A, B, and C. Like when building a bank ramp, the first step is to cut the sidewalls, or templates, for the ramp. The templates on curving ramps are also called transitions. Cutting a curve on a piece of wood can be pretty tricky, and before you start, there are a couple of things you need to consider.

A radius is the distance from the center point to the edge of a circle. So you have to choose a radius length whenever you cut a transition. For your small jump ramp, we recommend an 11-foot (3.35 m) radius.

Before you cut the template, you need to draw out your transition. Drawing a perfectly curving transition is actually more simple than it sounds. All it takes is a pencil and an 11-foot (3.35 m) length of string. The 11-foot (3.35 m) string acts as your 11-foot (3.35 m) radius.

Step A: Cutting the Transitions

Cutting the transitions is the most difficult part of the process. But once you get this done, the rest is relatively easy.

1

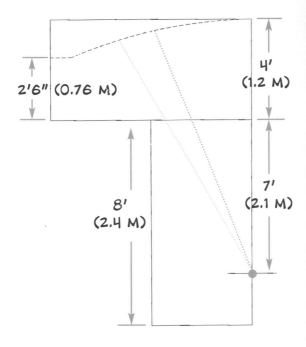

2'6" (0.76 M)

4' (1.2 M)

8' (2.4 M)

7' (2.1 M)

Lay your ¾-inch-thick (19 mm) sheet of plywood flat on the ground. Then take one of your ⅜-inch-thick (9.5 mm) sheets and lay it perpendicular to the first sheet.

Now measure exactly 7 feet (2.13 m) down the outer edge of the ⅜-inch (9.5 mm) plywood and make a pencil mark near the edge. Use your hammer to tack a nail in on this mark so it's partially sticking out. Then tie the pencil to one end of the string, and tie the other end to the nail. If you do everything right, the string and pencil should reach exactly to the upper right corner of the ¾-inch-thick (19 mm) plywood.

Starting at this upper right corner, pull tight on the string and drag the pencil's tip across the plywood toward the left. If it goes smoothly, you'll end up with a perfectly curved pencil line.

From the bottom corners of the ¾-inch (19 mm) plywood, measure up 2 feet 6 inches (0.76 m) and make a mark at each point. Then use a two-by-four as a straight edge to form the top of your jump ramp.

2

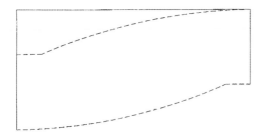

Making a smoothly curving cut in plywood can be challenging. Get an adult to do it using an electrical power saw. Some people use jigsaws to cut curves, but we recommend using a regular circular saw for a cleaner, steadier cut.

Instead of repeating the whole process with the string and pencil, after you've cut your first template, simply flip it over on the same piece of plywood and trace the shape with a pencil. That way, your two transitions will be identical. Cut out your second template.

(continued on page 42)

Step B: Assembling the Ramp's Frame

3

Cut each of the two-by-fours into two sections that are 3 feet 10½ inches (1.18 m) long sections. Sandwich the two templates together. Use your tape measure to measure the transition. Divide this number by 10. The number you get will be the amount of space between each joist. Make 10 marks along the outer edge of the transition where the joists will go.

Begin screwing the 3-foot-10½-inch-long (1.18 m) two-by-four cross braces in at each set of marks. Use the longer 2½-inch (64 mm) screws. The skinny edge of the two-by-four should be perfectly even with the edge of the transition.

You should screw from the outside face of the template, putting in two screws on each end (a total of four screws for each two-by-four). For extra stability, place one cross brace on the bottom edge of the ramp, flush with the ground, and one at the top back corner.

Step C: Attaching the Surface

4 Use your tape measure to measure the distance from the top of the ramp down the transition to the tip. This measurement will be slightly different depending on the size of the radius you used to cut the templates. Using the measurement you took in the first step, measure and cut both pieces of ⅜-inch-thick (9.5 mm) plywood, and also your sheet of Masonite, so that they'll all fit perfectly up the length of the ramp's transition.

Now begin attaching the first sheet of ⅜-inch (9.5 mm) plywood to the frame. Using the screw heads in the sidewalls as a guide, draw a straight line across the top of the plywood, exactly above several of the cross supports. Use this line as a guide for drilling in the screws, so that each screw will actually catch on the two-by-four cross supports below. (Note: You have to bend the plywood to the curve of the ramp. If you have trouble bending the plywood, or it starts to break, try soaking it in water for about half an hour.) Repeat the last step with your second piece of ⅜-inch (9.5 mm) plywood. See page 44 for the finished drawing.

JUMP RAMP

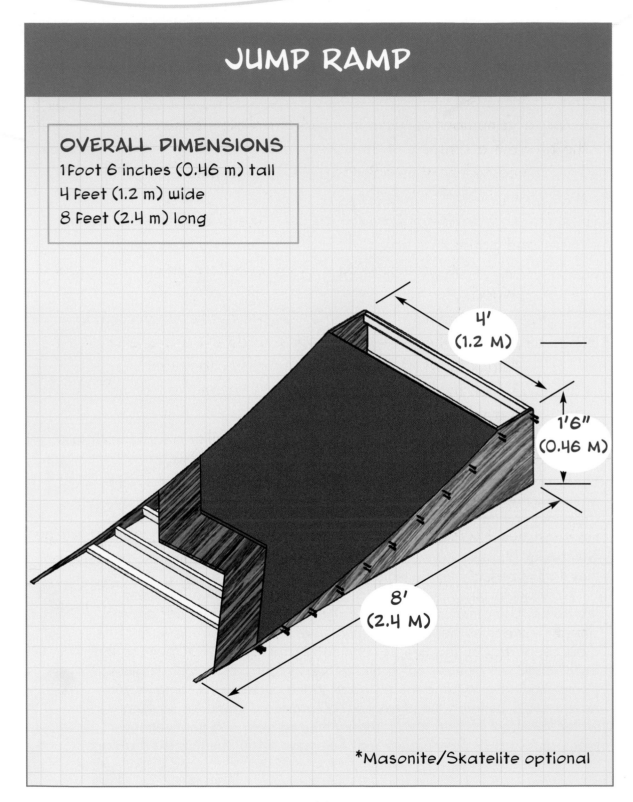

OVERALL DIMENSIONS
1 Foot 6 inches (0.46 m) tall
4 Feet (1.2 m) wide
8 Feet (2.4 m) long

4'
(1.2 M)

1'6"
(0.46 M)

8'
(2.4 M)

*Masonite/Skatelite optional

GLOSSARY

air Any of a number of tricks in which the skater is launched into the air from a ramp.

caulk A heavy-duty glue that carpenters use to piece together large pieces of wood.

coping The metal piping placed on the edge of a ramp to allow for slides and grinds.

countersinking A process of making screws flush on the surface of a piece of wood.

grind Any of a number of tricks in which the trucks, or the metal devices that the wheels are attached to, slide over a surface.

kick flip A trick in which the skateboard flips widthwise.

manual A trick in which the skater balances on the back wheels, similar to a wheelie.

Masonite A type of wood, chosen for its durability and smoothness, that is used to surface a ramp.

ollie A trick in which the skater and board become airborne.

Phillips-head screwdriver A screwdriver designed to screw Phillips-head screws, which have grooves in the shape of a plus sign.

plywood A type of wood used to construct the frames of most ramps.

Skatelite A material similar to Masonite that is used to surface ramps.

speed square A triangular tool for measuring perpendicular lines and corners.

warpage The amount that wood bends because of moisture.

FOR MORE INFORMATION

Royal Plywood Company
14171 East Park Place
Cerritos, CA 90703
(562) 404-2989
e-mail: customerservice@royalplywood.com
Web site: http://www.royalplywood.com

Skatelite World Headquarters
624 East 15th Avenue
Tacoma, WA 98421
(888) 383-5533
e-mail: skatelite@richlite.com
Web site: http://www.skatelite.com

Surface Industries
24 West 5th Street, Suite #203
Tempe, AZ 85281
(480) 894-9376
e-mail: info@surfaceindustries.com
Web site: http://www.surfaceindustries.com

Web Sites

Due to the changing nature of Internet links, the Rosen Publishing Group, Inc., has developed an online list of Web sites related to the subject of this book. This site is updated regularly. Please use this link to access the list:

http://www.rosenlinks.com/skgu/awob

FOR FURTHER READING

Brooke, Michael. *The Concrete Wave: The History of Skateboarding.* Toronto: Warwick Publishing, 1999.

Davis, Gary, and Craig Steycyk. *Dysfunctional.* Corte Madera, CA: Gingko Press, 1999.

Doeden, Matt. *Skateparks: Grab Your Skateboard.* Mankato, MN: Capstone Press, 2002.

Thatcher, Kevin. *How to Build Skateboard Ramps, Halfpipes, Boxes, Bowls, and More.* San Francisco: High Speed Productions, 2001.

Thatcher, Kevin. *Thrasher Ramp Plans.* San Francisco: High Speed Productions, 2003.

Thrasher Magazine. *Thrasher: Insane Terrain.* New York: Universe Publishing, 2001.

BIBLIOGRAPHY

Thatcher, Kevin. *How to Build Skateboard Ramps, Halfpipes, Boxes, Bowls, and More.* San Francisco: High Speed Productions, 2001.

Thatcher, Kevin. *Thrasher Ramp Plans.* San Francisco: High Speed Productions, 2003.

INDEX

About the Author

Justin Hocking lives and skateboards in New York City. He is also an editor of the book *Life and Limb: Skateboarders Write from the Deep End*, published in 2004 by Soft Skull Press.

Credits

Cover (inset) © Ronnie Kaufman/Corbis; p. 4 © Paul A. Souders/Corbis; pp. 8, 11 photo by Cindy Reiman; all working drawings by Yumas Donato.

Designer: Les Kanturek; Editor: Nicholas Croce